PRINCEWILL LAGANG

Marriage Miracles: Christian Couples' Stories of Faith

Contents

1

The Seed of Faith

The morning sun bathed the quaint, little chapel in a warm, golden hue, casting a comforting glow on the faces of the worshippers who gathered there. It was a Sunday, a day of reflection and gratitude, and the small town of Willowbrook had come alive with the sound of church bells and hymns echoing through the rolling hills. As the congregation settled into the wooden pews, there was a palpable sense of anticipation. Today marked the beginning of a remarkable journey into the lives of Christian couples whose marriages were infused with faith so strong it defied explanation.

Pastor Daniel stood at the pulpit, his voice gentle yet resolute as he began the service. His sermon was aptly titled 'The Seed of Faith,' and the congregation leaned in, eager to absorb the wisdom that would unfold.

In the first row, Sarah and James sat, their hands interlocked, their eyes locked in a loving gaze. Their story, a powerful testament to the resilience of love, faith, and the miraculous ways in which God's grace could manifest, was one of the first we would explore.

The Early Days

Sarah and James had met as teenagers. Theirs was a classic small-town romance that had blossomed in the shadow of the church steeple. High school sweethearts, they had navigated the trials of youth, growing up together while embracing their faith. Their love, though strong, was not without challenges.

The seed of their faith was planted firmly in their childhoods. Sarah's parents, devout Christians, had raised her to believe in the power of prayer. Her father, a carpenter, often spoke of the beauty of creation, emphasizing that the same God who made the universe watched over their lives. For James, his parents had been equally devout. His mother was a Sunday school teacher, and his father a deacon in the church. The family's evenings were often spent reading the Bible, and James had grown up understanding the importance of living according to God's will.

The Storm

The test of their faith came in the form of a storm, both literal and metaphorical. On a cold winter evening, a catastrophic snowstorm had struck Willowbrook, isolating the town from the outside world. The storm was fierce, knocking out power lines, closing roads, and creating a desperate situation. James and Sarah, recently married, were trapped in their home.

With supplies running low and the temperature dropping, they found themselves facing a grim reality. Sarah was expecting their first child, and the situation grew direr with each passing day. They prayed for help, but it seemed their pleas were met with silence.

The situation became dire, and they were on the brink of despair when a knock on the door shattered the silence. It was their neighbor, Mr. Miller, who had risked his own life to bring them food and blankets. He had heard their prayers and felt led to help.

The Miracle

It was this moment, Pastor Daniel explained, that marked the true test of their faith. Their prayers weren't answered in the way they had hoped, but God had sent a guardian angel in the form of their neighbor. They had realized that faith wasn't just about receiving what they wanted but also trusting in God's plan and opening themselves to His guidance.

As Sarah and James looked back on that difficult time, they saw it as a turning point in their lives. Their faith had grown stronger, and their love had deepened. They understood that miracles didn't always come in grand, dramatic forms but often in the kindness and love of others. Their marriage had become a living testament to the power of faith and the beauty of God's grace.

The Journey Ahead

The congregation listened, their hearts stirred by the story of Sarah and James. As the service came to an end, Pastor Daniel left the congregation with a thought: "The seed of faith is planted in the darkest of moments. It's up to us to nurture it with love, trust, and a belief that God's plan is always greater than our own."

In "Marriage Miracles: Christian Couples' Stories of Faith," we will delve into the lives of couples like Sarah and James, who have weathered storms and found strength in their faith. Their stories serve as a beacon of hope and a reminder that miracles are not rare events but an integral part of the journey for those who believe.

This is just the beginning of our journey, a glimpse into the lives of these remarkable couples, and there are many more stories of faith and love waiting to be shared in the chapters that follow.

2

Anchored in Hope

In the tranquil town of Graceville, nestled among rolling hills and sun-kissed meadows, lived Rebecca and Samuel, a couple whose lives were a testament to the power of hope in the face of adversity. Their story, which unfolded over the years, was one of unwavering faith, perseverance, and the realization that, even in the darkest of times, love and hope could be the beacons guiding them through life's turbulent waters.

The Blossoming of Love

Rebecca and Samuel met as university students at Graceville's Christian College. Their romance was born out of a shared passion for service and their unwavering faith in God. Both had volunteered for mission trips, spreading the message of hope and love to communities in need, and it was during one of these trips that their friendship blossomed into love.

Their love was a testament to the belief that a strong foundation of faith could forge an unbreakable bond. Their shared values and spiritual connection served as the cornerstone of their relationship, and they knew that their love was anchored in something greater than themselves.

A World Unraveled

As life unfolded and they married, the couple embarked on a journey filled with dreams of service and adventure. They saw their marriage as a vessel to carry hope to those in need, much like the ships that set sail from the nearby harbor.

Their world took an unexpected turn when Samuel was diagnosed with a life-threatening illness. The diagnosis was a harsh tempest, threatening to capsize their dreams and aspirations. It was a test of their faith like none other, as they faced the possibility of losing the one they loved most.

Anchored in Hope

Amid the storm that had engulfed their lives, Rebecca and Samuel clung to their faith with unwavering determination. Their love for each other and their belief in God's plan served as an anchor that kept them from being swept away by despair. It was during this trying period that their faith bore fruit, revealing itself as a wellspring of strength and hope.

As they navigated the difficult waters of treatment and recovery, they found support from their church community, who wrapped them in a cocoon of love and prayer. Their hope, which had once been an abstract concept, became tangible and embodied in the kindness of those around them.

The Miracle of Healing

Rebecca and Samuel's story took a miraculous turn as Samuel's health began to improve against all odds. Doctors marveled at his recovery, and the couple saw it as a divine miracle. The experience had transformed their lives and deepened their understanding of faith, love, and hope.

They realized that hope was not merely a feeling but a force of nature—a force that could sustain them even in the face of life's most formidable challenges. Their marriage, once tested by fire, emerged stronger and more resilient, a shining example of the power of faith and hope.

Lessons of Love and Hope

In "Marriage Miracles: Christian Couples' Stories of Faith," the story of Rebecca and Samuel stands as a poignant reminder that hope can be a lifeline in the darkest of times. Their marriage, rooted in love and faith, showcases the profound transformation that can occur when we face adversity with unwavering hope.

As you journey through the pages of this book, you will encounter more couples whose lives have been touched by the divine hand of hope. Each story is a testament to the enduring power of faith and the miracles that can emerge from the depths of despair.

Rebecca and Samuel's story is but one of the many beacons of light in this collection, and their lives are a testament to the enduring power of hope and the belief that, with faith as our guide, we can weather any storm.

3

The Power of Forgiveness

In the heart of the picturesque town of Serenityville, Emily and Daniel's love story unfolded as a remarkable narrative of faith, forgiveness, and the profound healing power of love. Theirs was a tale that demonstrated that, in the realm of marriage, forgiveness could be the bridge over the deepest chasms of despair.

A Love Forged in Trials

Emily and Daniel, both born and raised in Serenityville, had crossed paths during their teenage years. They were drawn together by their shared love for music and an unwavering belief in the importance of community service. Their bond grew stronger as they navigated the challenging terrain of high school, with their faith providing an anchor in the turbulent seas of adolescence.

Their love story was a beautiful symphony of faith and friendship that culminated in their marriage, celebrated with a joyous ceremony in the local church they both held dear. It was a day that felt blessed by the presence of a higher power, a reminder that their faith was the cornerstone of their union.

The Unraveling

Their life together began like a harmonious melody, but as the years passed, they faced discordant notes that tested their love. A financial crisis, compounded by unexpected job losses and mounting debts, strained their marriage. The walls of their home, once filled with laughter and love, echoed with frustration and sorrow.

Emily and Daniel's faith, which had brought them together, was now being tested to its limits. They found themselves questioning God's plan as they struggled to make ends meet. Bitterness and resentment crept into their relationship, creating a divide that seemed insurmountable.

A Journey to Forgiveness

But Emily and Daniel's story was far from over. In the darkest hour of their marriage, they encountered a transformative lesson in the power of forgiveness. It was during a Sunday service at their church that they heard a sermon on the healing grace of forgiveness. The message resonated with them deeply, and they realized that they needed to let go of their resentment and anger.

Their journey toward forgiveness was arduous, filled with tearful conversations and moments of vulnerability. They learned that forgiveness wasn't a one-time act but an ongoing process, and they were committed to making it a central part of their lives.

The Miraculous Transformation

As Emily and Daniel forgave each other and sought God's guidance in rebuilding their marriage, they witnessed a miraculous transformation. Their financial situation didn't miraculously improve, but the atmosphere at home changed. Their relationship was infused with a newfound sense of grace, understanding, and unconditional love.

Forgiveness, it turned out, was the bridge that helped them overcome their struggles. It allowed them to let go of their past grievances and focus on building a future together. Their faith, once strained, became a source of strength, guiding them towards reconciliation and a renewed commitment to each other.

Lessons of Love and Forgiveness

Emily and Daniel's story in "Marriage Miracles: Christian Couples' Stories of Faith" stands as a powerful testament to the transformative power of forgiveness. Their marriage was not exempt from the storms of life, but their faith and willingness to forgive breathed new life into their love.

As you explore the stories of other couples in this book, you'll find that the ability to forgive is a common thread among those who have experienced miraculous transformations in their relationships. Forgiveness, they discovered, is the balm that heals wounds, rekindles love, and restores faith in the power of love's enduring grace.

Emily and Daniel's journey teaches us that forgiveness is a divine gift that has the potential to mend even the most broken of hearts and renew the bonds of love in a marriage.

4

Through Sickness and Health

Nestled in the rolling countryside of Harmony Grove, Sarah and Michael's love story unfolded as a poignant narrative of faith, resilience, and unwavering commitment, emphasizing that true love knows no bounds, especially in the face of illness.

A Love Blossoming in Youth

Sarah and Michael's journey began as childhood friends in Harmony Grove. They were inseparable throughout their school years, their bond strengthened by shared adventures in the woods and the fields surrounding their town. Their faith grew side by side as they attended the local church, learning the values of love, compassion, and service to others.

Their love story emerged naturally, like a gentle stream finding its course. Their wedding, celebrated in the very church where they had been friends and confidants, was an event filled with promise and unwavering devotion.

The Unexpected Diagnosis

Years after their marriage, Sarah fell ill unexpectedly. It was a diagnosis that shook the foundations of their marriage—Sarah was suffering from a rare and severe illness. The couple, once accustomed to facing life's challenges together, found themselves embarking on a journey of medical treatments, uncertainty, and anguish.

Their faith, which had been a source of strength and comfort, was now put to the test. Michael, once a pillar of unwavering support, found himself struggling to come to terms with his wife's illness. Sarah, in the midst of her own pain and fear, clung to her faith, praying for the strength to endure her suffering.

A Promise to Persevere

As Sarah's health deteriorated and the burdens of her illness weighed on both of them, the promise they had made on their wedding day—to stand by each other through sickness and health—took on new meaning. Michael grappled with the overwhelming responsibility of caring for his wife, all while trying to maintain their home and faith.

Their journey was marked by moments of despair, but through it all, their love remained resolute. They found solace in the companionship and support of their church community, who prayed for them and extended a helping hand in their time of need.

The Power of Unconditional Love

Sarah and Michael's story was an exploration of the transformative power of unconditional love. They discovered that love was not bound by the limitations of health, nor was it diminished by suffering. In the darkest hours, they clung to their faith, seeking strength in the belief that God had a purpose for their journey.

Through prayer, resilience, and the support of their loved ones, Sarah's condition began to improve. It was a testament to the miraculous nature of healing and the unbreakable bond between them. Their love had grown deeper, their faith stronger, and their commitment unshakable.

Lessons of Love and Resilience

Sarah and Michael's story, featured in "Marriage Miracles: Christian Couples' Stories of Faith," serves as a reminder that love knows no boundaries and that faith can provide strength in the face of even the most daunting challenges.

As you delve deeper into the narratives of other couples in this book, you'll find that their stories share a common thread of unwavering commitment and love in the face of adversity. Their experiences underscore the profound truth that faith can be a guiding light through the darkest of times, and love can be an anchor in the storm of life's challenges.

Sarah and Michael's journey teaches us that love, tested by the trials of life, can emerge stronger and more enduring. Theirs is a story of resilience, unwavering faith, and the beauty of love that transcends all obstacles.

5

Rebuilding Trust

In the charming town of Hopeville, Grace and John's love story unfolded as a compelling narrative of faith, forgiveness, and the challenging but ultimately rewarding journey of rebuilding trust in a marriage that had weathered the storms of betrayal.

A Love Born in Faith

Grace and John's paths crossed at Hopeville's picturesque chapel during a Sunday service. Their shared faith and passion for service to their community brought them together. Their love, built on a foundation of shared values and spirituality, was a testament to the belief that faith could unite even the most unlikely of hearts.

Their marriage, celebrated in the same chapel where they first met, was a day filled with hope and promise. Friends and family gathered to witness the union of two souls who believed that their love was a gift from a higher power.

A Crisis of Trust

Their marital journey took an unexpected turn when Grace discovered that John had betrayed her trust. The revelation of infidelity shattered her world, leaving her feeling broken and vulnerable. Their faith, once a source of strength and unity, now seemed like a distant memory.

The path ahead was fraught with challenges. Grace grappled with feelings of anger, betrayal, and a profound loss of trust in the man she had believed to be her rock. John, overwhelmed with guilt and regret, sought forgiveness and reconciliation, but the road to rebuilding trust would be arduous.

The Journey to Forgiveness

As Grace and John faced the tumultuous seas of betrayal, they turned to their faith for guidance. They sought the wisdom of their church community and spent hours in prayer, searching for a path to healing. They discovered that true forgiveness was a process that required patience and understanding.

Grace began the difficult journey of forgiving John. Her faith became a wellspring of strength, enabling her to offer the grace and mercy she had once felt was impossible. John, in turn, took responsibility for his actions and actively worked to rebuild the trust he had shattered.

A Love Rekindled

Grace and John's story was not marked by an immediate return to bliss. It was a journey filled with moments of doubt, anger, and pain. However, as they traversed the rocky terrain of forgiveness, they discovered that love could, indeed, find its way back.

Through unwavering faith and a commitment to rebuilding trust, Grace and John saw a transformation in their marriage. Their love, tested by fire, emerged stronger, deeper, and more resilient. The lessons they had learned about forgiveness and trust had not only saved their marriage but had also drawn them closer to God and to each other.

Lessons of Love and Redemption

Grace and John's story in "Marriage Miracles: Christian Couples' Stories of Faith" stands as a powerful testament to the potential for redemption and renewal in the face of betrayal. Their marriage had weathered the storm of mistrust, and their faith had guided them toward forgiveness and healing.

As you explore the stories of other couples in this book, you'll discover that the power of faith, forgiveness, and the ability to rebuild trust are common threads in relationships that have withstood the test of adversity. Grace and John's journey serves as a reminder that love, once tested, can emerge stronger and more enduring, and that faith is a compass guiding us toward the path of forgiveness and redemption.

Their story teaches us that, even in the darkest moments of betrayal, love has the capacity to shine as a beacon of hope and renewal.

6

Love Across Generations

In the tranquil neighborhood of Generations Grove, the love story of Evelyn and William unfolded as a heartwarming narrative of faith, family, and the enduring power of love across the generations.

A Love Blossoming Through Time

Evelyn and William's paths crossed in the heart of Generations Grove. Their story began in a charming library where they both spent countless hours lost in books and conversations about faith, family, and their shared dreams for the future. Their bond deepened over the years, as they found in each other not only partners in love but kindred spirits in faith.

Their marriage, held in the same library where they had first met, was a celebration of a love that had grown through time. Surrounded by their children, grandchildren, and friends, they knew that their faith and love were the guiding stars of their enduring union.

A Test of Patience and Faith

As the years passed, Evelyn and William faced a challenge that would test the very core of their faith and love. William was diagnosed with a debilitating illness, one that slowly robbed him of his physical abilities. The active and vibrant man Evelyn had known for decades was now confined to a wheelchair, and the burden of care weighed heavily on her.

Evelyn's faith, which had always been a source of strength, seemed to waver under the weight of their circumstances. She questioned why God would allow this suffering in their later years, and William, facing his own physical limitations, struggled with a sense of helplessness.

A Testament to Unconditional Love

Evelyn and William's journey through this trying period was marked by unwavering love and a renewed commitment to their faith. Their family, including their children and grandchildren, rallied around them, offering support, love, and care. Their faith community became a source of solace and inspiration, reminding them that God's love was ever-present, even in the face of suffering.

Evelyn's role as a caregiver was a testament to the enduring power of love. Her selflessness and devotion to William showcased the depth of her commitment, transcending physical limitations. And William, though bound by his wheelchair, remained a pillar of strength and a source of wisdom for his family, reminding them of the importance of faith, hope, and love.

The Legacy of Love

As the years passed and William's condition remained challenging, Evelyn and William discovered that their love was not defined by the trials they faced. Their enduring faith and love had left an indelible mark on their family. Their children and grandchildren were inspired by their example, learning that love could be a wellspring of strength in the face of life's challenges.

Evelyn and William's story, featured in "Marriage Miracles: Christian Couples' Stories of Faith," is a testament to the enduring power of love, faith, and family. Their marriage, spanning generations, reminds us that love is not defined by the passage of time but by the depth of devotion and the strength of faith.

Their story teaches us that even in the most challenging circumstances, love can be a beacon of hope and inspiration, passing down from generation to generation as a testament to the enduring power of faith and family.

7

Resilience in the Storm

In the coastal town of Sea Breeze Harbor, the love story of Rebecca and James unfolds as a tale of faith, resilience, and the strength of a marriage that faced the trials of nature and life's uncertainties head-on.

A Love Anchored in Faith

Rebecca and James, both residents of Sea Breeze Harbor, shared a deep love for the ocean and the spiritual connection they found near the shore. Their faith was intertwined with the rhythms of the sea, and their love for each other was a testament to the belief that faith could anchor two souls even in the midst of life's storms.

Their wedding, held on the sandy shores of their beloved beach, was a celebration of their love and their shared commitment to each other and to the higher power they believed watched over them.

A Life by the Sea

Rebecca and James built their life by the sea, operating a small fishing business that provided for their family and connected them to the ebb and flow of the ocean. Their days were marked by the beauty of the coastal town and the serenity of their faith, as they attended the local church and found solace in the hymns and prayers offered by their congregation.

Their life was seemingly idyllic, but as the residents of Sea Breeze Harbor knew all too well, nature could be a force to be reckoned with. When a powerful hurricane threatened their town, their faith and resilience were put to the ultimate test.

The Storm

As the hurricane approached Sea Breeze Harbor, Rebecca and James faced the harsh reality of their vulnerability. They evacuated their home, seeking shelter with family, and joined their neighbors in praying for the safety of their town. When they returned, the destruction was heartbreaking. Their home and livelihood had been swept away by the powerful storm.

It was a test of faith like no other. In the midst of the wreckage, they faced uncertainty, grief, and a profound sense of loss. But their faith, which had sustained them through the joys and challenges of life, remained unshaken.

Rebuilding and Renewal

Rebecca and James' story was not marked by defeat but by resilience and renewal. Their faith, combined with the support of their church and community, provided them with the strength to rebuild their lives and their business from the ground up. They learned that even in the face of adversity, the power of faith could be a guiding light.

As they rebuilt their home and business, their love emerged stronger than ever. They saw the storm not as a harbinger of despair but as a catalyst for growth. Their faith in God's plan had weathered the hurricane, and they now saw that their marriage, like their coastal town, could withstand the trials of life.

Lessons of Resilience and Faith

Rebecca and James' story, featured in "Marriage Miracles: Christian Couples' Stories of Faith," serves as a powerful reminder of the resilience that faith can provide in the face of life's most daunting challenges. Their marriage, tested by the fury of nature, emerged stronger and more resolute.

As you explore the stories of other couples in this book, you'll find that the power of faith and resilience is a common thread in relationships that have weathered the storms of life. Rebecca and James' journey teaches us that even when the tempests of life threaten to overwhelm us, faith can be an anchor of strength and resilience, guiding us through the darkest of storms.

8

Embracing Differences

In the bustling city of Harmony Haven, the love story of Maria and Carlos unfolds as a beautiful narrative of faith, understanding, and the powerful bond of a marriage that bridged cultural and linguistic divides.

A Love Uniting Cultures

Maria and Carlos were drawn together in the heart of Harmony Haven, a city known for its rich cultural diversity. Maria had grown up in a devout Christian family with deep roots in the city, while Carlos had immigrated from a Latin American country, bringing with him a vibrant culture and a strong Catholic faith.

Their love story was a fusion of cultures and faiths. They met through a mutual friend, and from the very beginning, they recognized that their connection was something special. Their wedding, held in a church that seamlessly blended their Christian and Catholic traditions, was a testament to their shared faith and their determination to embrace each other's differences.

A Language of Love

The first challenge in their marriage came in the form of a language barrier. Maria, a native English speaker, and Carlos, a Spanish-speaking immigrant, often found communication to be a source of frustration. The misunderstandings and miscommunications tested their patience and tolerance.

Through their faith and their commitment to each other, they embarked on a journey to bridge this linguistic divide. Maria began learning Spanish, while Carlos improved his English. They discovered that love could transcend language and that faith could guide them through the challenges of cultural differences.

Navigating Traditions

The differences in their cultural backgrounds also presented unique challenges. Their family traditions and religious practices often clashed, leading to tensions in their relationship. Maria's family had strong Christian values, while Carlos's family adhered to Catholic traditions. They realized that faith and family were integral parts of their lives, and they had to find a way to harmonize their differences.

Through open dialogue, compromise, and a deep understanding of each other's backgrounds, they navigated the intricate web of traditions, weaving a tapestry that incorporated the best of both worlds. Their faith remained at the core of their union, and they found that love could thrive in the midst of cultural diversity.

Lessons of Understanding and Faith

Maria and Carlos's story, featured in "Marriage Miracles: Christian Couples' Stories of Faith," offers a profound lesson in embracing differences. Their marriage transcended language and cultural divides, proving that faith and love could conquer even the most formidable challenges.

As you delve into the stories of other couples in this book, you'll find that the ability to understand and accept each other's differences is a common thread among relationships that have overcome adversity. Maria and Carlos's journey teaches us that faith can be a bridge that connects people from different backgrounds, allowing them to build a marriage that celebrates the beauty of diversity.

Their story serves as a reminder that love and faith are universal languages, capable of uniting hearts that are open to understanding, tolerance, and the appreciation of the differences that make each of us unique.

9

Love's Second Chance

In the quiet town of Renewal Ridge, the love story of Elizabeth and Robert unfolded as a poignant narrative of faith, transformation, and the profound beauty of a second chance at love.

A Love That Overcame Loss

Elizabeth and Robert, both widowed and grieving, found solace in each other's company during a support group for those who had lost their spouses. Their shared experiences of loss formed a strong bond, and the empathy they extended to each other was a testament to their faith in the healing power of love.

As their friendship deepened, they discovered that faith was a powerful force that could transcend the darkest of times. They decided to marry in a small, intimate ceremony that celebrated the hope and faith that had brought them together. It was a union of hearts that had learned to love again after the pain of loss.

Navigating Blended Families

Both Elizabeth and Robert brought children from their previous marriages into their new family. The challenges of blending their families were daunting, as each child had their own experiences and emotions to navigate. Their faith was instrumental in guiding them through this complex transition.

They realized that faith, which had played a significant role in their own healing, could be a beacon of hope for their children. They fostered an environment of understanding, empathy, and shared faith, helping their children come to terms with the changes in their lives. Their marriage became a living testament to the power of faith and love to transform and heal.

The Beauty of Renewal

As the years passed, Elizabeth and Robert's love flourished. They found joy in nurturing their blended family, attending church together, and engaging in community service. Their marriage became a testament to the beauty of renewal and the incredible transformation that love and faith could bring.

They realized that their union was not a replacement for their previous marriages but a new chapter that celebrated the lessons learned from their past. The second chance at love was a precious gift, one that they embraced with gratitude and faith.

Lessons of Healing and Faith

Elizabeth and Robert's story, featured in "Marriage Miracles: Christian Couples' Stories of Faith," serves as a reminder of the healing power of love and faith, even in the face of profound loss. Their marriage was a beacon of hope for those who had experienced the pain of losing a spouse.

As you explore the stories of other couples in this book, you'll find that love and faith can provide a second chance at happiness, even in the face of life's most devastating challenges. Elizabeth and Robert's journey teaches us that, with faith as our guide, we can heal and find love again, celebrating the beauty of renewal in our lives and relationships.

10

Building a Legacy of Love

In the peaceful village of Legacy's Embrace, the love story of Sarah and John unfolds as an inspiring narrative of faith, service, and the enduring commitment to building a legacy of love that would span generations.

A Foundation of Faith

Sarah and John's love story began when they were teenagers in Legacy's Embrace. They met in the local church and shared a deep and abiding faith. Their courtship was a testament to their shared values, and their wedding, held in the same church, was a joyous celebration of their love and their commitment to a life of faith and service.

Their faith wasn't just a part of their relationship; it was the cornerstone that their love was built upon. Their belief in God's plan for their lives guided their journey together.

A Life of Service

From the beginning, Sarah and John shared a passion for service. They dedicated their lives to helping others, often volunteering together in their community. Their faith was the driving force behind their desire to make a positive impact on the lives of those less fortunate.

As the years passed, they expanded their family and continued their mission of service. Their home became a haven for people in need, and their children grew up witnessing the power of faith and love in action.

Navigating Life's Challenges

The path of love and service was not without its trials. Sarah and John faced financial difficulties, health setbacks, and personal losses that would test the resilience of their marriage. Yet, their faith remained unshaken.

Through prayer and unwavering belief in God's purpose, they navigated life's challenges together. Their children, now young adults, drew inspiration from their parents' faith, using it as a compass for their own journeys.

A Legacy of Love

As Sarah and John looked back on their lives, they realized that their marriage had been a source of joy and fulfillment. Their love had not only enriched their own lives but had also touched the lives of countless others in their community.

Their children, inspired by the legacy of love and faith their parents had built, continued the tradition of service. The family's commitment to faith and love had become a living legacy, one that would be passed down to future generations.

Lessons of Service and Faith

Sarah and John's story, featured in "Marriage Miracles: Christian Couples'

Stories of Faith," serves as a powerful reminder of the enduring impact of love and service. Their marriage was not just a union of two hearts; it was a partnership in faith, a journey of love and service that created a legacy of hope for the generations that would follow.

As you explore the stories of other couples in this book, you'll discover that love and faith have the power to create a lasting impact, not only in the lives of the couple themselves but in the lives of those they touch through their acts of service and commitment to a higher purpose. Sarah and John's journey teaches us that a legacy of love and faith is a gift that keeps on giving, inspiring others to live a life of purpose and devotion to those in need.

11

Sustaining Love in Retirement

In the peaceful retirement community of Graceful Meadows, the love story of Margaret and Edward unfolds as a heartwarming narrative of faith, togetherness, and the enduring love that blossomed in their golden years.

A Love Rekindled

Margaret and Edward's paths had crossed during their youth, but they had lost touch over the years. It wasn't until they both found themselves living in the serenity of Graceful Meadows that their connection was reignited.

Their love was a rekindling of an old flame, a second chance at love that brought them both comfort and joy in their retirement years. Their shared faith was a cornerstone of their relationship, uniting them in a bond that was stronger than ever before.

The Gift of Time

Retirement was a gift of time, and Margaret and Edward seized this opportunity to deepen their faith and their love. They spent their days volunteering at the local church, organizing community events, and offering their support to those in need.

Their faith provided them with a sense of purpose in their retirement, reminding them that they had the power to make a positive impact in their community. Their love for each other and their shared commitment to service brought them closer together.

Navigating Health Challenges

As the years passed, Margaret and Edward faced health challenges that often accompany old age. Edward's memory began to wane, and Margaret's mobility was restricted by arthritis. The challenges of aging could have strained their love, but instead, they leaned on their faith to navigate these difficulties.

Their bond of faith and love remained steadfast. They chose to focus on the moments they still had together, cherishing their shared memories and the love that had grown and deepened with time.

A Love That Endures

Margaret and Edward's story is a testament to the enduring nature of love and faith. Their retirement years, far from being a time of idleness, were marked by an active commitment to their faith and their community.

Their journey is a reminder that love can not only withstand the tests of time and health but can also flourish in the later stages of life. Their love was like fine wine, maturing and becoming more refined with each passing year.

Lessons of Love and Devotion

Margaret and Edward's story, featured in "Marriage Miracles: Christian Couples' Stories of Faith," serves as a poignant reminder that love and faith are not confined by age or health. Their marriage was a testament to the enduring power of love and the profound impact of service in one's community.

As you delve into the stories of other couples in this book, you'll find that love and faith can be a source of strength and inspiration, even in the later years of life. Margaret and Edward's journey teaches us that retirement can be a time of renewed purpose and devotion, a season of love that continues to grow and flourish, reminding us that love and faith can sustain us throughout the various stages of our lives.

12

The Dance of Marriage

In the vibrant town of Harmony Springs, the love story of Lily and David unfolds as an inspiring narrative of faith, partnership, and the intricate dance of a marriage that endures the changing rhythms of life.

A Love Born of Music

Lily and David's paths converged through their shared love for music. They met in the town's community choir and quickly discovered a harmonious connection that extended beyond their vocal talents. Their shared faith in God's divine orchestration of life drew them closer, and their love bloomed like a well-composed symphony.

Their wedding day, marked by melodies and hymns, was a joyful celebration of their love and their faith. They saw their union as a beautiful dance, a metaphor for the partnership they were about to embark on.

The Choreography of Life

As Lily and David navigated the complex dance of marriage, they encountered various steps and rhythms. The early years were a joyful waltz, filled with laughter, adventure, and the anticipation of their future together. But as they stepped into the middle years, they encountered the challenges of balancing careers, raising children, and finding time for each other.

Their faith became the guiding choreographer of their marriage. They leaned on God's wisdom and sought support from their church community to navigate the complexities of life. With faith as their foundation, they found the strength to harmonize their responsibilities and nurture their love.

The Dance of Renewal

As they moved into the later years, Lily and David faced the ebb and flow of life's changes. Their children left home, and they began to grapple with the reality of aging parents and health concerns. The dance of their marriage became a delicate tango, filled with moments of tenderness and vulnerability.

Yet, their faith remained unwavering, and they used it to sustain their love. Through prayer and communication, they learned to embrace the dance of renewal in their marriage. They recognized that love, like a well-choreographed routine, could adapt and evolve as they grew older.

The Dance of Legacy

As they reflected on their journey, Lily and David realized that their marriage had created a beautiful legacy. Their love had impacted not only their family but also their community. Their faith had been the music that had guided their steps throughout their dance of marriage.

Their story is a testament to the enduring power of faith and partnership in the dance of marriage. It reminds us that, like a beautifully choreographed routine, love requires dedication, adaptability, and faith to endure the changing rhythms of life.

Lessons of Faith and Partnership

Lily and David's story, featured in "Marriage Miracles: Christian Couples' Stories of Faith," underscores the significance of faith and partnership in the enduring dance of marriage. Their journey teaches us that, with faith as our guide and a commitment to working in harmony with our partner, we can navigate the ever-changing steps of life's dance, creating a love that endures and leaves a lasting legacy for generations to come.

Book Title: Marriage Miracles: Christian Couples' Stories of Faith

Book Summary:

"Marriage Miracles: Christian Couples' Stories of Faith" is a poignant and inspiring collection of stories that celebrate the power of love, faith, and resilience in the context of Christian marriages. Each of the twelve chapters delves into the unique love story of a Christian couple, highlighting the challenges they faced and the role faith played in guiding them through life's trials.

The book explores various themes, including:

1. Love's Beginning: The journey of couples who found love in the most unexpected places, often as childhood friends who grew into lifelong partners through their shared faith.

2. Overcoming Adversity: Couples who navigated hardships, such as illness and financial struggles, while holding onto their faith and commitment to one another.

3. Rebuilding Trust: Stories of betrayal and forgiveness, where faith provided a path toward healing and restoring trust in the face of infidelity.

4. Resilience in the Storm: The unwavering love of couples who faced natural disasters and leaned on their faith to weather the storms, both literal and metaphorical.

5. Love Across Generations: Couples who bridged cultural and generational divides, highlighting the beauty of embracing differences and the role of faith in building unity.

6. Love's Second Chance: Love stories that began anew after the pain of losing a spouse, showing the transformative power of faith and the beauty of renewal.

7. Sustaining Love in Retirement: The exploration of enduring love in the golden years, where faith and service remained at the core of a loving partnership.

8. Building a Legacy of Love: Couples who dedicated their lives to service and left a lasting legacy of faith, love, and community impact.

9. The Dance of Marriage: A narrative of the intricate dance of marriage, with its various steps and rhythms, and the enduring role of faith in sustaining love through life's changes.

Each story is a testament to the remarkable ability of faith to guide couples through the trials and tribulations of married life, demonstrating that love can grow stronger with time and that the power of faith can sustain us even in the darkest of moments.

"Marriage Miracles: Christian Couples' Stories of Faith" is an inspirational and heartwarming compilation that illustrates the enduring power of love and faith in Christian marriages, serving as a source of hope and guidance for couples at every stage of their own marital journeys.

www.ingramcontent.com/pod-product-compliance
Lightning Source LLC
LaVergne TN
LVHW010947200726
843509LV00013B/2308